Around The World London 🇬🇧

Ashley Lee

ISBN
Hardcover: 978-1-969844-33-1
Paperback: 978-1-969844-32-4

Dedication

To all my little sweethearts around the world who may never leave their home country. I hope my books help you move through the world!

About the Author

Ashley Lee is a open minded writer who speaks in a straight forward and profound way when relating her thoughts and feelings to her readers. Writing has been a passion of hers for over 10 years. She is versatile in her writings and speaks from experience and from opinions, for feedback from her audience. Kids books is an area she likes to focus on giving her the platform to express herself in her own way to create a world of opportunity.

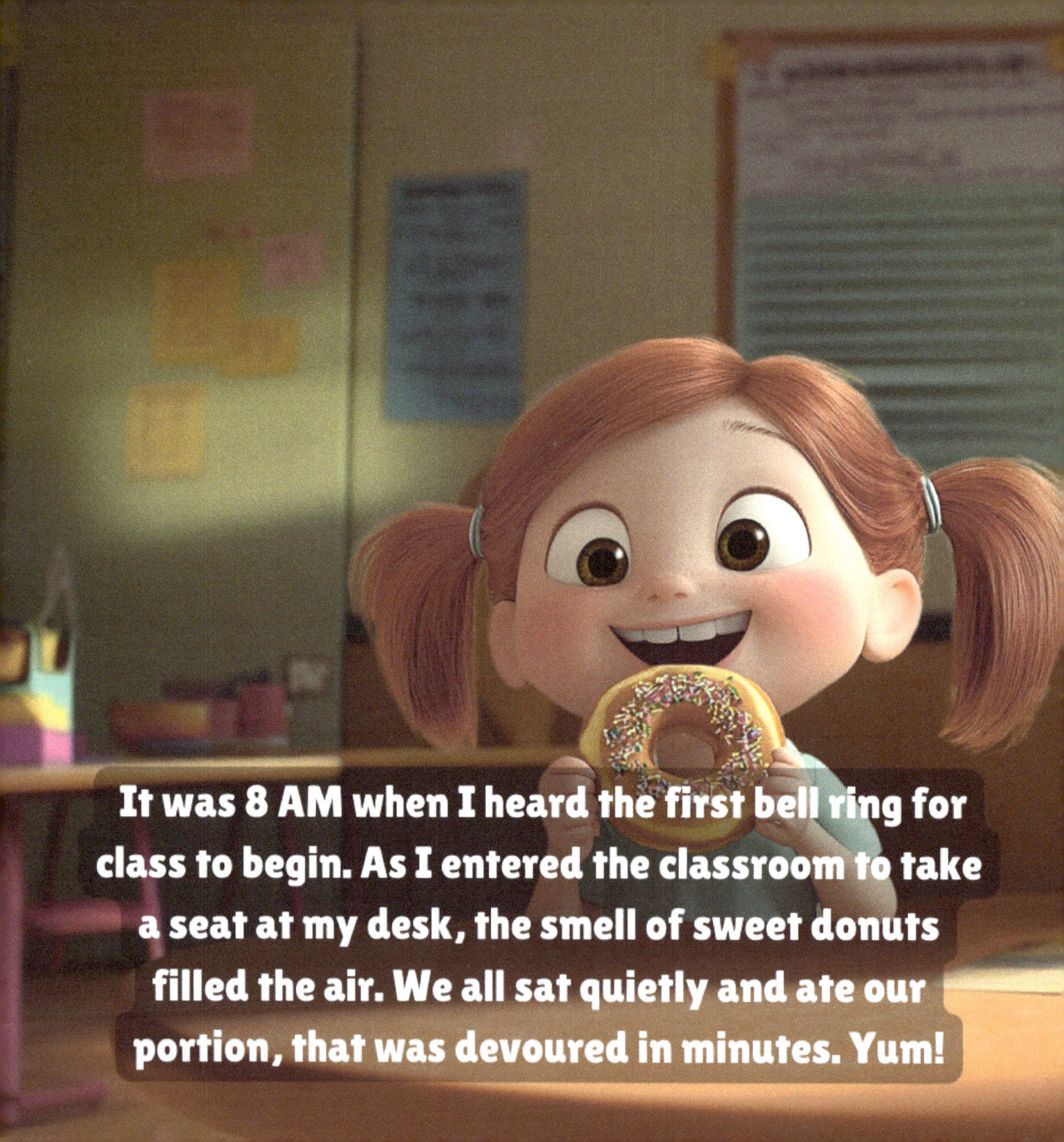

It was 8 AM when I heard the first bell ring for class to begin. As I entered the classroom to take a seat at my desk, the smell of sweet donuts filled the air. We all sat quietly and ate our portion, that was devoured in minutes. Yum!

Mandy, "here". Phence, "here". Nova, "present". We finished attendance and got into groups of 3 to finish our school trip worksheets then to go over our upcoming travel adventure.

"Who is going to be on their best behavior" said Ms. Madrid. "I am", the whole class said in unison. "My mom was born in Surrey, directly beneath London's borough" I said to my friends. "My dad was born in Jamaica. That's our next destination! I'm so happy to be able to visit both places my parents are from. I feel like i'm learning more about who I am".

London is the first place we'll travel to that's halfway around the world. This flight would take an average of around 9 hours. That's quite a long time for me to sit still. That's more than a whole day of school, on a plane! I started to feel a little anxious.

"Don't stress yourself Nova", Phence said with a grin. "I've got some Uno cards we can play to pass some time on our flight there".

We all got slightly lightheaded soon after take off, but our numerous games of Uno kept us occupied. After a few hours of gaming and watching movies, we decided to take a nap. We woke up to a meal of meatloaf, mashed potatoes and broccoli and one of the most beautiful landings I've seen so far.

For this trip, we settled ourselves on a nearby campsite to have the best experience possible. Here, they had rows of cabins and a large bonfire that groups of students from the campground gathered around during the day and night.

Did you know that London is considered a forest? According to U.N. definition. Any area that has at least 20% trees is considered a forest. Trees cover around 21% of the land making it an urban forest. In fact, 8.6 million people are known to live alongside 8.3 million trees.

We were lucky to come across some UK natives that gave us the most insight about the small city they lived in.

The smallest city in England is London. It's actually about 1.2 square miles in size otherwise known as the "square mile".

The London region, known as greater London, is further divided into the city of London and 32 London boroughs.

Black cabs are a very famous part of London culture, which you can see everywhere. But to become a black cab driver, is not so easy. Typically, the training last 2 to 4 years and candidates must memorize every single street in London. So you never have to worry about if your driver knows where they are going or pulling up to the wrong destination.

The UK isn't the only city in the world with London in it. The U.S.A. has 10, Canada and France both have one. There is even an asteroid called London.

Flying a kite is illegal in parks and certain public areas, the Metropolitan police areas or in any way that annoys other people. If you ever fly a kite in violation of the law, you risk receiving a fine of up to £500, that's a little over $630.

NO KITE
FLYING

Did you know that the clock in the tower is called Big Ben. In honor of the queen's diamond jubilee, the famed towers name was changed from clock tower to Elizabeth tower in 2012.

According to research, there are more than 300 languages spoken in London, making it the most linguistically diverse city in the world. The top 5 non—english languages reportedly spoken are Polish, Turkish, Bengali, French and Punjabi.

London was once the capital of six countries at the same time. In WWII, London served as the governing capital for other European countries, which were conquered by Germany. The leaders of Norway, Poland, Belgium, France and the Netherlands, stayed in London between 1939 and 1945.

We went exploring the city and came across a few more unique places, such as the Millennium Dome now call the O2, which is the largest building of its kind in the world.

The Shard standing at 309.6 meters is the tallest building in London. That's 72 stories.

We completed our evening admiring and riding the London Eye, which is 135 meters tall, that's 442 feet. It has a diameter of 120 meters, 393 feet. It has 32 capsules and a ride takes 30 minutes. The entire wheel weighs more than a 1000 tons. It gave us the most beautiful view of the city as if we were landing from the plane again.

We settled back at the camp around the fire, making smores while singing London Bridge and other old rhymes. Once again, I was opened up to another world of people and life learning experiences that I can take with me everywhere I go. I love my school.

www.ingramcontent.com/pod-product-compliance
Lightning Source LLC
Chambersburg PA
CBHW042343030426
42335CB00030B/3439